The POWER of IGNORANCE
The ignorance trap

DAVID H. SWENDSEN

To order additional copies of this book, contact:
Xlibris
1-888-795-4274
www.Xlibris.com
Orders@Xlibris.com

List Books by David H. Swendsen

	TITLE	DATE PUBLISHED	CLASSIFICATION (PUBLISHERS)
1.	BADGE IN THE WILDERNESS	1984	NON FICTION (STACKPOLE)
2.	A WILDERNESS WITHIN	1988	NON FICTION (XLIBRIS)
3.	FAULT ISLAND	2003	FICTION (OUTSKITS)
4.	LAST BREATH	2012	FICTION (CREATESPACE)
5.	A REAL NIGHTMARE	2015	FICTION (XLIBRIS)
6.	LEADERSHIP IN OUR LIVES	2014	NON FICTION (CREATESPACE)
7.	THE RESOURCE RACE	2015	NON FICTION (CREATESPACE)
8.	IT'S MIDNIGHT	2015	AUTOBIOGRAPHY OF A DOG (CREATESPACE)
9.	TAMING OUR VIOLENT WORLD	2016	NON FICTION (CREATESPACE)
10.	FROM HELL TO HEAVEN	2018	NON FICTION (AUTHORCENTRIX)

THE POWER OF IGNORANCE   **11/12/18 (sub title-The Ignorance Trap)**

(How ignorance can create power)

PROLOGUE

Almost every day our newspapers and magazines come up with articles and statements about the eye catching expressions: black power, white power, the power of the press, the power of suggestion, the power of numbers, the power of the spoken word, and even the power of persuasion. Our unrelenting television advertisements also constantly remind us of these life entering powers that affect us all as we confront the unexpected rapid changes that take place all around us in our fast moving lives.

As important as it is that we are aware of all of just how the above powers affect our lives, I believe there is another over whelming power that affects each and every one of us, regardless of age, health, wealth, or where we might call home on this heavily populated planet earth. There have been many articles and books written, and hundreds of interesting statements made by well- known persons throughout history, about this life-changing, important power. In this book I will attempt to explain just how I think the *power of ignorance* does affect each of us during our lifetimes. Having acquired and confronted my share of ignorance in my lifetime, I feel I am qualified to attempt to point out several of the significant effects of ignorance on our existence on this constantly changing planet. After looking into some definitions of *ignorance* and *ignorant,* I will discuss just how our periods of ignorance can make it possible for some of our LEADERS throughout the world to accumulate a great deal of *power.*

CHAPTER 1.
KINDS OF IGNORANCE and IGNORANCE QUOTES

There appears to be two kinds of ignorance or two kinds of ignorant people. A naively ignorant person is innocent of knowledge but can be open to learning. An aggressively ignorant person does not appear to like to feel ignorant and avoids learning–in that way, they become perpetual victims of the ignorance trap. This easy to fall into trap can overtake us about not knowing something. There are two ways in which we cannot know. First we can know that we do not know. Secondly and much worse, we are unaware that we do not know. This later case leads us into actions where we act in foolish ways without realizing that we are being foolish–the ignorance trap. This type of ignorance can lead to denial, and even when faced with real evidence, the aggressively ignorant may literally ignore the truth. This kind of ignorance can lead to real tragedies in a person's job, associations and family life, and it if enough people are trapped by their own ignorance a great deal of damage in the world can suddenly appear.

IGNORANCE QUOTES:

In her book "Armed & Magical, **Lisa Shearin** wrote---"Whoever said ignorance is bliss must have died a horrible death with a really surprised look on his face."

Dalai Lama- "Were ignorance is our master, there is no possibility of peace."

Dr. Wayne Dyer- International author wrote, "The highest form of ignorance is when you reject something you don't know anything about."

George Bernard Shaw, "Beware of false knowledge; it is more dangerous than ignorance."

A NAIVELY IGNORANT PERSON IS INNOCENT OF KNOWLEDGE BUT CAN BE OPEN TO
LEARNING. THIS PERSON MIGHT BE OPEN-MINDED ENOUGH TO TAKE THE CORKS OUT
OF HIS EARS, LEARN, AND BE ABLE TO CHANGE SOME OF HIS HABITUAL BAD HABITS
AND MOVE FORWARD IN HIS NEEDED ACTIONS TOWARD COMMON SENSE.

CHAPTER 2.

LIARS USE LIES TO GAIN THEIR POWER FROM THE IGNORANT

"Make the lie big, make it simple, keep saying it, and eventually they will believe. It is not the truth that matters but victory."

Adolf Hitler

Hitler was not alone in the telling of lies to gain the support of the German people in his plan to gain the power to destroy all the Jews in Germany. Hitler was also not alone in the telling of lies to gain the support of those he governed. Our history books and our everyday happenings are loaded with leader quotes that were actually lies. These untrue quotes got these leaders the attention and usually the backing they felt they needed to survive their leadership hectic rolls. Everyone lies, although those who tell "little white lies," do so, usually with no real intent to promote themselves or to harm anyone.

So what well known persons have lied in the past? Do presidents lie? George Washington appears to have always told the truth even if it got him in trouble. The moral of the story–Washington was a great leader because he would not lie, and all presidents are expected to be as honest as our founding father. Former Washington lobbyist Ed Uravic, who also teaches at Harrisburg University in Pennsylvania says, "Every president has not only lied at some time, but needs to lie to be effective."

Examples:

President Franklin Roosevelt- While preparing the country for World War II, told Americans in 1940, that "your boys are not going to be sent into any foreign wars."

President John F. Kennedy- In 1961 declared that **"I** have previously stated, and I repeat now, that the United States plans no military intervention in Cuba." All the while, he was planning an invasion of Cuba.

President Ronald Reagan- Told Americans in 1986, "We did not, I repeat, did not trade weapons or anything else (to Iran) for hostages, nor will we," four months before admitting that the U.S. had actually done what he denied.

President Abraham Lincoln-lied about whether he was negotiating with the South to end the war. "He also lied about where he stood about slavery," says Meg Mott, a professor of political theory at Marlboro

College in Vermont. Mott also said He played slave-holders against abolitionists. He had to lie to get people to follow him.

President George W. Bush- When defending his plans to invade Iraq. "America must not ignore the threat gathering against us. Facing clear evidence of peril, we cannot wait for the final proof, the smoking gun that could come in the form of a mushroom cloud." (claimed Iraq had nuclear weapons).

President William Clinton- He told the nation, "I did not have sexual relations with that woman." He later admitted this relationship but was not impeached.

President Richard Nixon- After it came to light that he had been involved in illegal activities, including wiretapping and harassment of political opponents in the Watergate scandal, Nixon lied and tried to cover up the misdeeds. The truth eventually came to light. He resigned before he could be impeached.

What is the definition of a lie? Webster gives several definitions:

1. "to make a statement or statements that one knows to be false, especially with intent to deceive."
2. "To give a false impression." "Anything that gives or is meant to give a false impression."
3. "To bring, put, accomplish, etc. by lying: As he lied himself into office."
4. "A thing said or done in lying; falsehood."
5. "To charge with telling a lie." "To prove to be false."
6. "Liar= a person who tells lies."

Webster's various definitions of what is a lie appears to open the door to just what did the person who told the lie expect to accomplish. Hitler's statements (lies) that he made he knew were without a doubt false and were definitely made with the intent to deceive, and also were made to gain him power. And in many cases he was using the power of ignorance, with his lies directed toward those Germans who really didn't understand all of his motives regarding his plan toward world domination.

Some of the statements that turned out to be untrue when made by a U.S. President, or made by some less prestigious leaders, might have been made to gain some support or acceptance for a stance they previously had taken regarding a pending controversy. These previous statements later proven to be untrue, and maybe made, when first made, gave a false impression, but now with more facts coming forward might not be classified as *lies to deceive*.

Quotes about lies and honesty:

Author Unknown- "If you want to ruin the truth, stretch it."

Abraham Lincoln- "No man has a good enough memory to make a successful liar."

Yiddish Proverb- "A half- truth is a whole lie."

Robert Brault, free-lance writer- "Every lie is two lies-the lie we tell others and the lie we tell ourselves to justify it."

Winston Churchill- "A lie gets halfway around the world before the truth has a chance to put its pants on."

Groucho Marx- "There is one way to find out if a man is honest- ask him. If he says yes, you know he is a crook."

Children from Iraq that suffered due to George Bush administration decision to go to war claiming Iraq was in possession of nuclear bombs. Even if against common sense.

US military in Iraq during the war in Iraq.

CHAPTER 3.

HOW BEING CREATURES OF HABIT MAKES US VULNERABLE

Ignorance and the power of ignorance is definitely not new to the world we live in. It has been in play since the beginning of time. Both the power of ignorance and the lack of intelligence regarding this power, rear their ugly heads almost every time someone suggests or tries to suggest a possible change in the way we humans do things.

As Human beings we tend to be creatures of habit. Leaders who are looking for any possible support can take advantage of this way of life and promise jobs, or money to those whose habits are fulfilled.

Hitler, when he made his lies and statements during his world takeover charge, understood the habits of the German people. He used this knowledge to move forward in his attack on the German Jews.

Hitler's early successes demonstrated is often much stronger than the power of truth or the power of fact. How is it possible that a group of supposedly well-meaning persons will suddenly rise up loudly against, or loudly for, some activity, maybe described as factually proven, maybe field tested, or maybe thought by some people to be needed badly? So suddenly, there is a plan to go for, or go against making a change to that activity. Being *creatures of habit* is often an activity that, "We have always done it that way" or instead, "we have never done it that way before." I also believe in another *unwritten rule* that we humans appear to live by. That rule is, that no matter what project or plan an individual proposes, or even starts to carry out, there will always be someone, or some group that will be against this new plan or project. I can think of no exception to this consistently pursued *ongoing rule.*

Part of why the power of ignorance, causes we humans to resist change, I believe is because we mostly live in our own little world. Few people really investigate a cause before they join in, for or against a suggested change. This probably is because we humans are such *creatures of habit. We* always sleep on the same side of the bed. We park our car in the same spot at work or at home (if possible). We buy our groceries and drugstore needs at the same stores every time we shop, almost without exception. We basically eat the same kinds of meals and partake in the same pre-dinner drink before our dinner. That is if we habitually have that drink or instead habitually refrain from drinking altogether. We take our showers or baths at the same time each day or week, and always use the same brand of soap and same brand of toothpaste to brush our teeth. We read the same newspapers and magazines at a specific time, or we don't read newspapers or magazines at all. We watch the same TV programs and follow the same sporting teams in the papers or on TV broadcasts, or maybe we have never been interested in sporting events. We put on our car seatbelts if we have developed that habit. We take the chance of being thrown from the car if involved in an accident if we have a habit of not hooking up our seatbelts.

Depending on our upbringing and what we *learned from our parents,* or what good or not so good examples our parents were to us, becomes an important ingredient in developing in each of the habits we might carry on for the rest of our lives. Where we live, our living conditions and the extent of our wealth or lack of wealth play a huge role in just what kind of habits make us what kind of human being we become. Lack of having two guiding parents gives ignorance a good foothold to enter into a child's existence and make his or her future financially more stressful and can often lead to illegal conduct.

Because we are such *creatures of habit we* don't really jump into the battle *until we believe a proposal appears to enter our way of life.* Even then few people really investigate a cause before they join in being for or against. Suddenly your neighbor is violently and definitely opposed to, or intensely for: capital punishment, the draft, more freeways, Obamacare, sex education, a new shopping center, long hair, short skirts, selling liquor on Sundays, or maybe just blacktopping the roads in front of his or her house. Why did the neighbor or his neighbor suddenly join the cause against black topping the street in front of *his* house? Why did someone write letters and call congressmen in an effort to get the town to allow selling liquor on Sundays, or instead be adamantly against selling liquor on Sunday? Why? Because everything we humans do becomes personal to us. For one neighbor the black-topping he believes will cost him money in taxes he doesn't think he should pay. While the other neighbor across the street has been after the town for years to get the job done and has gotten other neighbors to help get the paving accomplished.

I due believe there is an unwritten rule that many of we humans appear to live by. That rules IS: that no matter what the project or plan an individual or group or even starts to carry out, there will always be someone, or some group that will BE AGAINST this new plan or project. No matter how valid or needed the change seems to be the unwritten rule says NO!! Even if saying NO is against common sense.

The guy who really wanted the town to allow selling liquor on Sunday was part owner in a liquor store. It would certainly not be unusual for this guy to want to protect his business, and he certainly wouldn't understand any woman's individual reason for taking away his Sunday business. The woman who was adamantly opposed to Sunday liquor sales was because she was having a continuing problem with a son who has been arrested three times for driving while intoxicated, the last time on a Sunday. Does she believe it will protect her son from another driving while intoxication arrest? She thinks it will. Will it really cost the one neighbor money out of his pocket for the blacktopping? He assumes it will. Yes, we really are creatures of habit. But *suddenly there is an unusual happening* that we are personally involved in. Yes, then we might break a habit or two and because we are somewhat "ignorant" of all the circumstance, we may be convinced to suddenly become someone who now becomes a *"for or against."*

CHAPTER 4.

WAYS THAT LEADERS USE THE PUBLIC'S IGNORANCE TO GAIN POWER

Are all leaders political? So what does it mean to be political? Are all politicians seeking personal gain by scheming instead of gaining support by using salesmanship to gain support for their programs? So now what is salesmanship? Webster says salesmanship is the ability or skill at selling. So what is sales talk? Webster says sales talk is persuasion used in an attempt to sell something or any argument persuading someone to do something. Was Hitler a good salesman? Does everyone who strives to obtain a political office or leadership position, need to be a good sales person? I believe that history pretty much proves that presidents, mayors, governors, school superintendents, dictators, baseball and football managers, police chiefs, orchestra and band leaders, FBI directors, senators, town managers, chief cooks, company CEOs, and even some military generals and some judges have to be sales persons to get and to retain their leadership positions.

Do all of these leaders have to tell the truth during their sales pitch to get the backing they need to become the leader they are striving to become? Can promising certain rewards to those who are being asked to "buy" me and my programs gain followers? And again, do we agree that everybody lies? Do perspective followers sometimes really don't fully understand just what programs, true or false, they are asked to say yes to? And with this possible lack of understanding suddenly we now arrive at that dangerous and very common scene where *ignorance can and does create power.*

Again, if a perspective leader fully understands just how habitual we humans are in our way of life, and sells his or her programs in a way that captures our habits into his or her ambitions, this proposed leader has accomplished his or her sales talk.

If persons are unaware of, or not truly interested enough to investigate what is asked of them, doesn't mean they are truly an ignorant person, but are only ignorant of what is asked of them. This kind of ignorance can and very often does create power in the hands of our present or perspective leaders. And again the age old feeling that *having* can enter into how those persons respond to the sales talk that has been thrown at them, even if against common sense.

Good salesmanship by leaders whether they be a senator, police chief, football coach, school superintendent, or army captain, must be regularly carried out if they are going to be successful in their job. If in their supervisory role as a good leader they will not be successful if they continually take their group in a WRONG DIRECTION or become known as an AGANST-TER--- against all new ideas or new directional changes. Even for common sense.

Some of the other specific methods that some leaders and prospective leaders appear to use to gain backers for their campaign proposed programs:

1. They use *race and religious* differences that exist throughout the nation. These differences, often very volatile throughout the world, unfortunately have never been overcome. The United States has made some progress since the American Civil War (1861-1865) that abolished slavery and dissolved the Confederacy, but this nation and the rest of the world, have long way to go to overcome the

reluctance of all of its citizens to accept each other's race and religious differences. Unfortunately some politicians who are determined to become leaders in our society use this lack of acceptance of one another's race or religious differences to accomplish getting those persons on their bandwagon and achieve their goal of gaining votes, becoming elected, and acquiring leadership *power.* They accomplish this with ads and statements that are geared to gain support from some citizens who feel their lack of *having* wealth or education benefits or jobs or good jobs, is because of their race or religious beliefs. This politician's thirst for power is accomplished by strategically gaining the support of voters whose ignorance or lack of understanding makes them believe this politician will fulfill his or her promises to help them out of their poverty or lack of opportunity to have a better life.

2. There are leaders or potential leaders who promise *jobs,* undetectable *payoffs* or *programs* that his or her possible followers believe would benefit them. Some of these voters who may or may not fully understand the promises, do become followers, hoping to be rewarded for giving their support. Some of these voters do get rewarded if the leader they voted for is voted in and has now obtained that determined quest for power.

3. Sometimes leaders or potential leaders try to gain support by catering in the direction toward getting mostly *male* or in some cases mostly *female* support in their quest for election or program backers.

4. In all situations that a leader or potential leader, when needing to gain supporters, might very well delve into a fierce and often overwhelming *ad campaign,* paid for by well-healed *money-backers* who have much to make a business gain by the election or promised programs advocated by the campaigning person.

5. In recent 2016 political battles some candidates carried on extreme slighting of their opponents as to their past activities and sometimes completely false statements as to their opponents character.

In all of the above methods that a leader or potential leader might instigate to gain the power he or she is striving for, there is often a certain amount of questionable salesmanship used that will convince not only informed backers, but also a number of uninformed, *somewhat ignorant,* possible backers to get on the bandwagon.

CHAPTER 5.

What damage has the power of ignorance caused in the world in the past?

What some of the most recognized experts have said about damage caused by ignorance:

1. Martin Luther King Jr. - "Nothing in the world is more dangerous than sincere ignorance and conscientious stupidity."

2. George Benard Shaw- "Beware of false knowledge, it is more dangerous than ignorance."

3. Mario Balotelli (soccer player) "Racism springs from ignorance."

4. Emma Goldman (writer and political activist) "The most violent element in society is ignorance."

5. Confucius "Real knowledge is to know the extent of one's ignorance."

6. Henry Rollins (musician, writer, radio host)-"Weakness is what brings ignorance. Cheapness, racism, homophobia, desperation, cruelty, and brutality are things that keep a society chained to the ground, one foot nailed to the floor."

7. Henry David Thoreau - "True friendship can afford true knowledge. It does not depend on darkness and ignorance."

Some Leaders and money makers cause continued human suffering by using the power of ignorance to accomplish their goals:

1. The mistaken decision for the U.S. **to go to war in Iraq** because of the false assumption that Iraq had nuclear weapons was a *powerful ignorant* and disastrous decision by the **George W. Bush administration.**

2. Human beings are born with a wonderful gift of human intelligence. This helps develop a lifelong determination to succeed in our everyday affairs, such as to preserve our underlying health and to maintain our needed self-esteem. This intelligence mechanism enables us to be able to deal with most difficult situations. But when we put our faith and our goals in the hands of **any leader or proposed leader**, and that person lies to us or abandons us, it can send us down a path toward depression and a dangerous loss of self-esteem. We can now be overpowered by what I call *the* **ignorance trap.** Those persons who use this vulnerable population of depressed persons do a great deal of harm to the world's societies and needed progress in the world.

3. Failure for the US to logically continue to move ahead now in the battle to combat climate change. Calling "global warming" a hoax, is a frightening stance that **some politicians,** backed by **big money factions** and an **uncompromising US congress** continue to disregard the importance of controlling world CO2

emissions. This careless attitude jeopardizes our planet's present and future livable environment for today's citizens and citizens of tomorrow's world.

4. Failure of the **US congress** to pass needed firearms regulations. Backed by the leaders of the present **NRA,** who continue to strongly appose the passing of laws that would restrict the possession and use of certain firearms, continues to escalate the high rate of firearm deaths which occur in the USA every day.

The NRA continues to fight all agencies and citizen groups and congress, against the promotion of any sensible, needed firearms regulations. The NRA also continues to claim that the US government wants to take away all the firearms that are owned by US citizens. That is not true and never has been.

5. **Donald Trump** in his campaign to become the President of the US, claimed as president he would build a **wall** along the Mexican border that would be paid for by the Mexican government. He claimed this would stop illegal entry into the US by Muslim immigrants. **Trump** on November 13th stated that he would deport 2 to 3 million undocumented immigrants when he takes office. Now, as president, on January 26, 2017, he reaffirmed and signed documents to move forward on building the wall and still maintained that Mexico will pay for building the wall. This has seriously alienated the Mexican government. **Trump,** on that date also signed off allowing several controversial pipelines to begin further construction. He appears to be following his campaign promises. This action has alienated many American citizens who are trying to stop these intrusions into special lands that they believe are sacred. When the president of the United States continues to tell it's citizens that he doesn't believe in climate change or that our growing human populations are effecting our recent escalating violent storms, floods, hurricanes and tornados, while the vast majority of Americans and creditable worldwide scientists provide conclusive evidence that human being population's living styles and actions are causing our atmospheres and weather cycles to change dramatically. And the scientists claim by altering our present earthly living styles to a more thoughtful and caring state, our earth would still be livable for our children's children's children.

The Trump administation weakened the sacred MIGRATORY TREATY ACT in 2018 and also took away the protection of national park and refuge lands from oil drilling ventures. against common sense he also weakened regulations for pictured wildlife picture here.

Protected Bald Eagle

Protected Endangered Elephant

Protected Endangered Tiger

1. The war in Iraq cost many lives and left many towns in a devastated bombed out CONDITIION

2. Leaders who want to support and be surrounded by "BIG MONEY BUSINESSES" and who stomp down those who are trying to prepare for ONGOING AND FUTURE CLIMATE CHANGE, claim that CLIMATE CHANGE IS A HOAX, but when that so called hoax turns into a ignorant follower's disaster, the former follower falls into depression!

$$\$$$

Big money businesses are willing and able to invest in advertising and supporting those citizens who will follow a leader who also proclaims he is solidly backing the big money businesses. An example - the oil industry businesses.

THINGS CAN GO REALLY BAD

3. When a promising potential leader promises his "followers" and then lies his way out of his promises, for the followers it can be HELL AND DEPRESSION!!

4. The NRA does not support the passage of even sensible firearm laws.

As a leader and special agent with the government, I was disappointed with the NRA'S safety instruction.

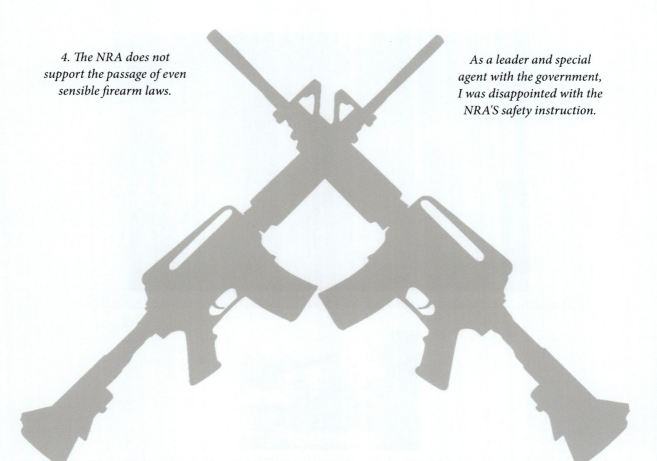

AK 47 AUTOMATIC RIFLE - NOT NEEDED BY CIVILIANS

National Park rangers being trained in the safe use of firearms.

5. *President Trump first claimed that CLIMATE CHANGE was a hoax. Later he stated that the following devastating weather related events were caused by nature's expected changing ways. He said, "Nature would probably change these ways back in the future?". But all in all, in the meantime, American citizens and their homes and lands across our country were being attacked by overwhelming CLIMATE CHANGE destruction elements that unquestionably were and are real, and not a "HOAX".*

UNITED STATES WILDFIRE, CALIFORNIA

UNITED STATES FLOOD, FLORIDA

UNITED STATES VOLCANO, HAWAII

UNITED STATES TORNADOS, NORTH CAROLINA

The world's earth exploring scientists give these example of needed changes:

A. We must control our earthly rising temperatures by lowering the atmosphere CO2 content. High temperatures cause droughts, crop failures, food less available, polar ice caps melting causing flooding of certain areas, which leads to an imbalance for wildlife and creates ocean fishless-plantless dead zones.

B. Stop the high rate of forest deforestation and instead plant more forests, especially the rain forests in South American. Trees extract groundwater which is released into the air.

C. Slow Pollution, which includes everything from liter on streets to garbage floating in the oceans. Slow down throwing away "STUFF." Recycle.

D. Stop the losses of Biodiversity–bee population increased. Donate to world wildlife fund and stop wildlife habitat destruction.

E. Discontinue the use of fertilizer that end up in oceans as was done near the Black Sea in Europe.

F. Explosive world population growth of last year was 7 billion, putting strain on water, food, well-being, space and sanity. Increase educating all humans about sensible food use against waste. Controlling population difficult but educating present inhabitants and new inhabitants is possible.

IF MORE OF THE WORLDS INHABITANTS BECAME EDUCATED AS TO THE A-F ABOVE SUGGESTIONS, THEIR WOULD BE LESS NEED TO BE SO UNCONCERNED ABOUT THE POWER OF IGNORANCE!!

A. Attempts to control the release of CO2 into the earth's atmosphere is a constant battle between many segments of industry and those agencies and countries who are attempting a needed cutback.

Clear cutting of the world's forests in countries like Brazil in South America and European low income countries causes worldwide droughts and with it a shortage of foods that humans need to survive.

These cut over forests lands no longer provide the world with oxygen and an atmosphere that fought against droughts and a decrease in the world's food supply.

C. Slow pollution/stop littering/recycle
OCEAN TRASH

Protecting the Pacific Ocean is an existential issue. The oceans sustain all life on Earth. Finding a practical pragmatic way to protect the Pacific Ocean is a most. A recent meeting in BALI with five southwest Asia countries was meant to help in driving sustainable seafood production in all five Asia countries and the United States. The initiative can help meet regional goals, create jobs, and protect the health of the ocean now, and for future generations. John Kerry attended this important meeting.

There are numerous dead zones in the oceans of mother earth that are filled with plastic, chemicals, and litter and trash that we citizen have dumped into our rivers and stream to get rid of this trash.

The valid scientists of the world tell we human beings of the world, that it is time to stop getting rid of our stuff and our trash by throwing it away, ocean bound. We dump it every day from our ships, from our homes, and from our businesses. Most goes into our streams and rivers headed ocean bound, where it ends up contaminating, deadening, and disrupting our OCEANS, OUR ULTIMATE KEY TO FUTURE LIFE ON EARTH.

REFUGE TRASH

OCEAN VIEW

IF THE HUMAN POPULATION FOLLOWS THE SCIENTIST'S GODLY ADVICE OUR WORLD'S OCEANS WILL CONTINUE TO REMAIN THE BEAUTIFUL WATERS THAT WE CONTINUE TO NEED AND BE IN LOVE WITH.

PROTECTED GRAY WOLF

PROTECTED TIGER

PROTECTED ELEPHANT

PROTECTED BALD EAGLE

E. Use proper discretion for disposal of chemicals and fertilizers that can end up in Earth's oceans.

F. After last year's population explosion growth of seven billion human beings, there is a severe need to increase educating humans regarding food waste and plans to slow further growth in the Earth's human population.

My first-hand experience with someone who demonstrated his own *ignorance and leadership power* to revamp the U.S. Fish and Wildlife Service, was former Secretary of the Interior, **James WATT: Watt** was appointed by former president Ronald Reagan. The day Watt took over the F&W agency he told its lifelong professional director to vacate his office immediately even though no new director was chosen for several months. Only days after Watt was named Secretary of the Interior by Reagan, Watt's "wise use" plans were laid out coldly in a closed circuit television statement to those of us who worked for the Department of Interior. Some of Watt's plans included subsidizing underground rock, shale oil development in the west which quickly turned out to be a costly blunder. His **oil exploration plans were briefly explained. These plans included designating National Wildlife Refuges, National Parks and NATIONAL FOREST LANDS AS TARGETS. TO OVERIDE** members of congress and environmental group's actions to stall Watt's drilling plans on federal lands he directed drillers **to drill diagonally into protected lands from nearby private lands.** Watt did not outline, in his television address to his newly acquired employees, his next planned moves which were: 1. Cut program funding, virtually strangling the endangered species and marine mammal programs. 2. Encourage Alaska to complete "wolf control" on federal parklands. 3. Attempt to lift the ban on oil drilling in sensitive marine sanctuaries off the California coast. 4. Open fragile seashore beaches to all-terrain vehicles. 5. Cut federal land purchases that, because of escalating costs, will never be actualized.

Watt then made former California Fish and Games Director, **Ray Arnet** as Assistant Secretary of the Interior. (Arnet, while in office was apprehended and paid a fine for shooting shore birds from a powerboat). Watt and Arnet systematically disabled the USF&WS, with their **"Wise Use, Let's use it policy."** Wildlife programs that protected wildlife and habitat were considered by Watt as outdated, and unrestricted use of the nation's resources now became Watt's program. Watt's ignorant "wise use" decisions to move into a drastic misuse and abuse of our nation's resources continues today to disrupted the lives of its citizens who must rely on the remaining critical resources to survive on this "shrinking" planet earth.

I was affected in both my professional and personal life by **Watt's** "wise use" of our nation's dwindling resources. I became one of the Special Agents in Charge of one of the thirteen law enforcement districts in the U.S. that were created in 1974 by Chief Special Agent, Clark Baven because the size of the previous districts were too large to do their job of cooperating efficiently with the many states within their district. Watt and his yes men came in and **cut back these law enforcement working districts** back to seven, making the good working relationships again more difficult. Six of the law enforcement district offices were closed and Agents-in-Charge in these offices who "did not possess Washington office experience" no longer had a job. My district office fortunately was not closed but as I had no Washington office experience I could no longer be in charge of my office. Jim Sheridan, my assistant was made Agent-in-Charge of our Boston office. I no longer had a job until a real leader, Region Director Howard Larson, appointed me regional special project officer in charge of law enforcement training of all refuge patrol officers in his thirteen state region. I was also designated as Agent-in-Charge of enforcement raids in the region and assist in raids carried out in the US.

Two of the national raids I was asked to become involved in were in the enforcement of the Migratory Bird Treaty Act, specifically in the protection of waterfowl in Pennsylvania, and The Endangered Species Act, protecting bald eagles in Montana. By using my raid vehicle and working with a Pennsylvania officer we were able to park within seventy-five yards from three duck hunters who were suspected of over bagging each time they went duck hunting. We clocked each duck killed and by which hunter for about an hour and one-half. We then checked out the ducks in their possession and also the bag of ducks they had hid in the grass near their blind. All three hunters were cited for possession of ten ducks over their limit, and their shot guns were seized. The most significant raid I was part of as a special project officer was when I was detailed to Montana to help provide security for a person and his property. He was providing safe storage for a large number of live confiscated bald eagles. This legal permit holder had informed the government about the illegal possession and sale of bald eagles that he became aware of while operating legally. The USFWS Agents followed up on his information and conducted a large-scaled raid that involved many state and international violations of transporting eagles from Canada into the United States. Federal court action was pending. My job with my raid vehicle and the assistance of other special agents, was to provide nighttime protection for the bald eagles, and the property owner, who had received threats concerning his cooperation with the authorities. The violators were prosecuted in several federal courts. The live eagles were returned to the wild, or, if unable to fly, turned over to licensed U.S. rehabilitation centers.

This change in my job responsibilities as a special project officer, actually forced me to move out of the Regional office to our sub-office at the Customs House that overlooked the Boston harbor. I no longer travelled into the Boston Regional office every day, instead I was on the road quite often to National Wildlife Refuges to teach refuge patrol officers, and to lead law enforcement raids in the region and to participate in raids in USF&WS raids that were nationwide.

In 1984 I retired from the USF&WS. At that time retirement at age fifty-five was mandatory. Because of the fact that I had been teaching wildlife law enforcement at several colleges when still a federal agent, those colleges asked me to start several courses on a regular basis. I taught several courses for about five years at the University of Massachusetts, Amherst and University of New Hampshire and Wauchsetts Community College, at Gardner, Ma.

In 1989 the National Park Service asked me to consider directing a 400 hour Pre-Park Ranger program at the University of Massachusetts, Amherst, through the Universities Continuing Education Department. With the help of thirty or more expert law enforcement instructors from various state and federal agencies each semester, I directed this program until 2010. This course, (Conservation Law Enforcement Training Program CLETP) received the UCEA OUTSTANDING PROGRAN AWARDS 2008-----FOR NON-CREDIT PROGRAMS -It was nominated by the University of Massachusetts, Amherst.

Bald eagles for sale from Canada

Overbag ducks killed by Pennsylvania hunters

In the chapters of this book I have attempted to describe with words and telling pictures, just how I believe some leaders make use of the ignorance, not common sense, displayed by some citizens, as a tool that will help the leaders gain POWER, and gain the followers they need to accomplish their proclaimed goals and programs. Hopefully, my lifelong experience with all kinds of leaders and having been a prior leader in law enforcement and education agencies, will make my experience helpful to those citizens who will then not be lead down a path where their IGNORANCE IS MADE USE OF BY AN UNRELIABLE, SELF CENTERED LEADER. Common sense and the recommendations of worldwide scientists should guide the citizens who exist on this earth in the right decision, in regard to managing and living with NATURE and WILD ANIMALS in their future existences on this Earth..

THE AUTHOR ENJOYING THE UNIQUE OUTDOORS OF ECUADOR!

David H. Swendsen is a retired resource law enforcement officer. He was a Wisconsin Conservation Warden for eight years and, after over twenty years of federal service, retired as the U.S. Fish and Wildlife Service Special-Agent-in-Charge of the six state Northeastern Region. After federal retirement, he taught resource law enforcement at the University of New Hampshire, Wachusetts Community College, and the University of Massachusetts at Amherst for over eighteen years. From 1989 to April of 2010 he taught and directed the National Park Service's Ranger Law Enforcement program, using over 50 selected instructors, at the university of Massachusetts at Amherst. A graduate of the University of Wisconsin, Madison, Swendsen has written several resource law enforcement books, including "Badge in the Wilderness", published by Stackpole in 1984, "A Wilderness Within", by Xlibris in 2009 and "Leadership In Our Lives", by CreateSpace in 2014. Swendsen is also the author of various novels, including "Fault Island", "A Real Nightmare", "Last Breath" and "It's Midnight". He currently resides in Acton, Ma.

Printed in the United States
By Bookmasters